YOUR KNOWLEDGE HAS VALUE

AF146240

- We will publish your bachelor's and master's thesis, essays and papers

- Your own eBook and book - sold worldwide in all relevant shops

- Earn money with each sale

Upload your text at www.GRIN.com and publish for free

Bibliographic information published by the German National Library:

The German National Library lists this publication in the National Bibliography; detailed bibliographic data are available on the Internet at http://dnb.dnb.de .

This book is copyright material and must not be copied, reproduced, transferred, distributed, leased, licensed or publicly performed or used in any way except as specifically permitted in writing by the publishers, as allowed under the terms and conditions under which it was purchased or as strictly permitted by applicable copyright law. Any unauthorized distribution or use of this text may be a direct infringement of the author s and publisher s rights and those responsible may be liable in law accordingly.

Imprint:

Copyright © 2014 GRIN Verlag
Print and binding: Books on Demand GmbH, Norderstedt Germany
ISBN: 9783668442061

This book at GRIN:

https://www.grin.com/document/359187

Musfirah Mohamad

Structure, Culture and Leadership Management. Organisational Behaviour Between Kamdar Sdn Bhd and the Sara Lee Corporation

GRIN Verlag

GRIN - Your knowledge has value

Since its foundation in 1998, GRIN has specialized in publishing academic texts by students, college teachers and other academics as e-book and printed book. The website www.grin.com is an ideal platform for presenting term papers, final papers, scientific essays, dissertations and specialist books.

Visit us on the internet:

http://www.grin.com/

http://www.facebook.com/grincom

http://www.twitter.com/grin_com

Content

Introduction

I was given a task to make a research on Kamdar Sdn Bhd and Sara Lee Corporation regarding their structure, culture, employee's behaviour, leadership style, and management approached in each of the organisation. Below are the information from my research.

Task 1

1.1) Critically examine these two organisations by comparing and contrasting:

a) their differing structure

The structure of Kamdar Sdn Bhd and Sara Lee Corporation is same which is using product structure, division of product or product departmentalization. Both of these products use the same structure which is every divisional manager is given responsibility for the product or product line, with authority with personnel different function.

According to businessdictironary.com, *product departmentalization refers to the internal process performed by a corporation of dividing its business activities up according to the type of goods or services produced. Product departmentalization typically groups tasks related to a particular product or product line under one senior manager who specializes in that aspect of the company's business.* (Product departmentalization : BusinessDictionary)

Example of product structure or product departmentalization :

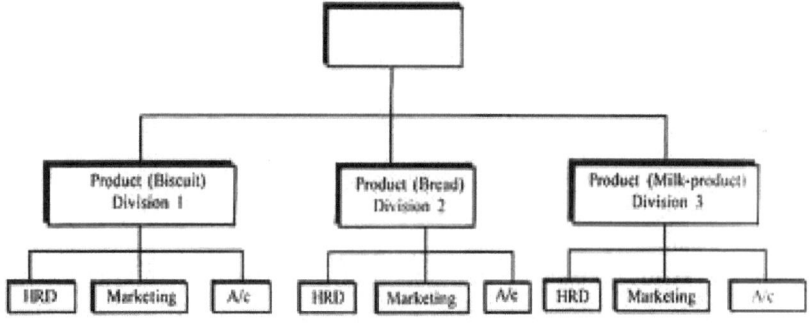

This structure gives focus on individual products, which may be especially appropriate if different products have different problems and concerns. The issue of focus is important because it determines the priorities people will have, and the way they think about those priorities. Each group can be run as a separate profit centre. Based on this way, healthy competition and rivalry can be developed between 'teams' which can help motivation and productivity. It is also flexible in that poorly performing groups can be closed down without too much disruption to the rest of the organisation. Co-operation between teams will improve where it is in the interests of both teams to do so.

Characteristic	Kamdar Sdn Bhd	Sara Lee Corporation
Structure	Product structure / Product departmentalization.	Product structure / Product departmentalization.
Product	Quality and garment products. Textile fabric, furnishing fabric, in-house design garment for ladies, men and children clothes, Indian clothing and school uniforms.	Food, beverage, household and body care.
Task	Every divisional manager in Kamdar Sdn Bhd will manage each product for example textile fabric, there will be Marketing Manager, R&D Manager Financial Manager, Economic management and Public Service management.	Every divisional manager of Sara Lee Corporation will manage the organization based on division of product. For example, there will be Marketing Manager, R&D Manager and Management Accountant under the household product.
Authority	Over personnel of different function.	Over personnel of different function.

b) their differing culture

Kamdar Sdn Bhd and Sara Lee Corporation have different culture in organisation. For Kamdar Sdn Bhd they use power culture and Sara Lee Corporation use task culture.

Characteristics	Kamdar Sdn Bhd	Sara Lee Corporation
Culture	Power culture.	Task structure.
Changes in culture	Permanent.	Temporary.

Authority	All employees have chances to make any suggestions and recommendations but the leader or owner have the authority in making decision for the organization.	Basically, it performs in a team. Everyone is empowered to make decision to complete particular tasks and leader will be the mentor.

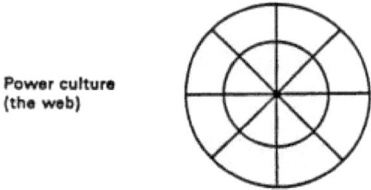

Power culture (the web)

According to businesscasestudies.co.uk, "*a power culture is one based on the dominance of one or a small number of individuals within an organisation. They make the key decisions for the organisation. This sort of power culture may exist in a small business or part of a larger business.*" (Corporate and organisational structure : The Times 100)

For example, *the massive institutions in the USA, run as a small family business at the top and known as 'robber barons'. Power is concentrated in a small area, the centre of which is the wheel or the centre of the web. Power radiates out from the centre, usually a key personality, to others in the family who send information down to either departments, functions or units. The important point to note is that, because power and decision-making is concentrated in so few hands, the strategists and key family members create situations which others have to implement. It is difficult for others outside the 'family network' to influence events. The ability of the power culture to adapt to changes in the environment is very much determined by the perception and ability of those who occupy the positions of power within it. The power culture has more faith in individuals than committees and can either change very rapidly and adapt or 'fail to see the need for change' and die.*" (Lindsay Sherwin)

In Kamdar Sdn Bhd, they use power culture whereby the decision making is centralized. Here, it means all the employees have given chances to make any suggestions and recommendations in their business organisation but the final decision will be made by manager or owner. The person who makes the decision must have the ability to influence others. Basically, the decision maker is always choosing by seniority or someone who is close to the business organisation and can be trusted. For example, Jayesh R Kamdar is the Executive Director of Kamdar Berhad so he has the right to make decision because the key executives applied power culture. In this type of culture, decisions can be made quickly as there is little consultation. However lack of consultation could mean that a firm is unable to take advantage of the skills and experience of its workforce then it could even lead to employees feeling demotivated and high staff turnover.

Next, this business organisation is an inherent business and the change of culture is permanent. Below is the example of the key executive of Kamdar :

KEY EXECUTIVES	
HAMENDRA A/L B.M. KAMDAR	Vice Chairman
M. CHANDRASEGARAN A/L S. MURUGASU	Secretary
SECK WAH LIM	Secretary
KAMAL KUMAR KISHORCHANDRA KAMDAR	Managing Director
EMAM MOHD HANIFF BIN EMAM MOHD HUSSAIN	Board Of Directors

(Kamdar Group (M) Berhad | Malaysia : Internet securities Inc.)

By applying the power culture, a person should has the characteristics of a leader in making decision such as based on personality, adaptable and informal, small size which the leader have direct communication with all employees and good personal relations. Let say, the Executive Director of Kamdar has made a wise and fast decision regarding the business organisation. This shows he has a good personality. His decision can influence and convince the employees and they will try to second the decision. A wise decision will lead to make the organisation perform well. Another example is Kak Ton's products. Her products can success in market because of her personality in promoting the product itself. Employees will attract to cooperate in providing the product and customer will attract to buy it.

Task culture (lattice)

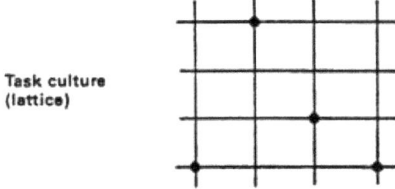

5

Based on businesscasestudies.co.uk, it explained that task culture *"exist when teams are formed to complete particular tasks. A distinct team culture develops, and because the team is empowered to make decisions, task cultures can be creative."*

According to lindsay-sherwin.co.uk defined task culture as the *"organisations which are involved in extensive research and development activities they are much more dynamic. They are constantly subject to change and have to create temporary task teams to meet their future needs. Information and expertise are the skills that are of value here. The culture is represented best by a net or lattice work. There is close liaison between departments, functions and specialities, liaison, communication and integration are the means whereby the organisation can anticipate and adapt to change quickly. Influence in this team culture is based upon expertise and up-to-date information where the culture is most in tune with results. The dangers for this culture exist when there is a restriction in resources causing it to become more power' or 'role' orientated."* (Culture-Handy :Lindsay Sherwin)

Task culture is based on team work from different departments. This type of culture is more like a team work based and staff which has different tasks to complete whether it is internal or external project. A team need to know the problem and have a goal to achieve.

To achieve the organisation goals, Sara Lee Corporation applied task culture in making decision, the expert workers in their field and a small team is formed on the basis of capability rather than seniority or status. The power and authority are distributed to the right people at the appropriate level of the organisation. This kind of task in temporary and it will finish when the task is successfully complete. For example, if Sara Lee Corporation wants to make promotion regarding their body care product so a team is formed to give suggestion and recommendation. Everyone in a team is empowered to make for decision making in order to achieve the goal. They may feel valued because they have selected for the team and there is a sense of achievement when the team complete the task successfully. It may also allow teams to be more creative when problem solving. In making decision based on task culture, a person need to have team based which is no dominant or clear leader, get the job done, expertise and talent, job satisfaction and many more.

1.2) Discuss how far Kamdar Sdn Bhd and Sara Lee Corporation structure and culture can bring impact on the performance of the business.

The impact on the performance of the business for Kamdar Sdn Bhd and Sara Lee Corporation can be seen by observing the advantage and disadvantage through the structure and culture of their organisation. Both Kamdar Sdn Bhd and Sara Lee Corporation applied same structure which is product structure and different culture for business organisation. Kamdar Sdn Bhd applied power culture while Sara Lee Corporation applied task culture.

Advantages and disadvantages based on structure.

Advantages of product structure for Kamdar Sdn Bhd and Sara Lee Corporation

Individual managers of Kamdar Sdn Bhd and Sara Lee Corporation can be held accountable for the profitability of individual products. Next, they also could be expertise in doing their work. For example, when the salesperson of both companies will be trained to sell a specific product, they will be more expertise and offer better services to the customers. In addition, the different function activities and efforts required to make and sell each product can be co-ordinated and integrated by the divisional or product manager.

Disadvantages of product structure for Kamdar Sdn Bhd and Sara Lee Corporation

Conversely to the advantages, product structure also has disadvantages. It is good by applying the product structure because a person will be expertise in their career. But, product structure will increase the overhead costs and managerial complexity for the organisation. Then, it can prohibit Kamdar Sdn Bhd and Sara Lee Corporation from achieving company-wide goals since each unit operates on its own.

Advantages and disadvantages based on culture.

Advantages of power culture for Kamdar Sdn Bhd

There are several advantages of power culture. Firstly, it will unify individual effort behind the vision of the leader. Manager or owner of Kamdar Sdn Bhd can move quickly in the market and make rapid internal changes. Based on this power culture, employees can leverage the knowledge, wisdom and talent of the leader. Last but not least, it can provide direction and certainty; reduce conflict and confusion in times of emergency. So, it is quiet importing by applying power structure.

Disadvantages of power culture for Kamdar Sdn Bhd

"Employees give the boss's wishes the highest priority, even when it interferes with important work. Then, employees are afraid to give bad news to the boss and they do not question the leaders even when they are seen to be wrong. Therefore, employees with power break rules with impunity and take special privileges. Then, information is a source of personal power and is restricted to friends and allies and employees are promoted by being loyal to those in power even when they are not especially competent." (Organisational structure)

Advantage of task culture for Sara Lee Corporation

Task culture also has some advantages in organisation. It brings unity of effort toward mutually valued goals within the team or organisation. It can reduce need for controls on individuals of Sara Lee Corporation. Then, the task culture will bring high internal motivation for the team exists. Next, task culture can give maximum utilization of Sara Lee Corporation members' talents. It also will produce high self-esteem for organisational members and rapid learning and problem solving within organisation. Lastly, task culture will build rapid adaptation to change.

Disadvantages of task culture for Sara Lee Corporation

Task culture can bring negative impact towards Sara Lee Corporation. Employees in the organisation will believe so much in what they are doing that the end comes to justify the means. Then, they will become intolerant of personal needs, and they sacrifice family, social life and health for work. The group members will talk only to themselves and become isolated from others and from reality. In addition, the group only cooperates internally, which others see as arrogant and competitive because dissent and criticism are stifled. The group member of Sara Lee Corporation will has difficulty correcting its own errors. Last but not least, their commitment to excellent at any cost could lead to waste and inefficiency.

1.3) What are the factors that could influence the employee's (Kamdar Sdn Bhd and Sara Lee Corporation) behaviour at work?

In order to manage people, we have to understand them first. If we understand why they behave like that, we are able to manage or change their behaviour. But, human behaviour is not easy to describe because everyone is different behave with time, circumstance and people.

Kamdar Sdn Bhd and Sara Lee Corporation have some factors that could influence the employee's behaviour at work. In individual behaviour at work, there are included personality, perception, attitude, ability and aptitude, conflict stress and change. Let say, the behaviour's employees of Kamdar Sdn Bhd and Sara Lee Corporation can be seen through their personality. Personality shows the total pattern of characteristics ways of thinking, feeling and behaving that constitute the individual distinctive method of relating to the environment.

'**Personality** *encompasses the relatively stable feelings, thoughts, and behavioral patterns a person has. Our personality differentiates us from other people, and understanding someone's personality gives us clues about how that person is likely to act and feel in a variety of situations. In order to effectively manage organizational behavior, an understanding of different employees' personalities is helpful. Having this knowledge is also useful for placing people in jobs and organizations."* (New Charter University, 2011-2014)

One of the personality characteristics is the big five factors. Psychologists have converged many personality regarding the structure and concept of personality. The five factors can be comprised as OCEAN which is Openness, Conscientiousness, Extraversion, Agreeableness and Neuroticism.

For openness, it describes an individual's pro active seeking an appreciation of experience for its own sake. Employees in Kamdar Sdn Bhd and Sara Lee Corporation which has this factor will be more emotions, adventurous and has high imagination in working. Employee who has high in openness seems to thrive in situations that require being flexible and learning new things. They are highly motivated to learn new skills, and they do well in training settings. Then, conscientiousness describes how organised, motivated, achievement oriented and dependable. So, if the employee has this characteristic they will be more cautiousness, discipline and have sense of duty when working. Employee also will have the achievement to strive in order to achieve the company's target. Conscientious people have higher levels of motivation to perform, lower levels of turnover, lower levels of absenteeism, and higher levels of safety performance at work. It is good for both companies when they have employees like this because it can establish a good trait to have for entrepreneurs.

For extraversion, it describes how energetic the person is especially when they deal with others. Employees always be more friendly, assertive, cheerful and excited when they are working. Basically, they actively seek information and feedback, and build effective relationships, which helps with their adjustment. Extraverts are also found to be happier at work, which may be because of the relationships they build with the people around them and their relative. Next is agreeableness. Agreeableness describes a person's attitudes toward others. If employees in textile fabric, furnishing fabric, in-house design garment for ladies, men and children clothes, Indian clothing and school uniforms have these characteristics they will be trusted, have cooperation and morality in doing their work. Normally, agreeable people may be a valuable addition to their teams and may be effective leaders because they create a fair environment when they are in leadership positions.

Lastly is neuroticism. It measures the different ways people have of reacting emotionally to pressure and stressful circumstance. Being high in neuroticism seems to be harmful to one's career, as they have lower levels of career success. They will be anger, depression, anxious and immoderate.

Task 2

2.1) Compare the effectiveness of leadership style that had been applied in Kamdar Sdn Bhd and Sara Lee Corporation.

By observing the structure and culture of Kamdar Sdn Bhd and Sara Lee Corporation, I have carried out the leadership style use for both of the companies. Kamdar Sdn Bhd use autocratic leadership style while Sara Lee Corporation applied democratic leadership style. Kamdar use autocratic leadership style because they applied power culture in their company. All decisions will be made by the leader or the owner and the members did not have the right to make decision. They just have the right to give suggestion and recommendation. Sara Lee Corporation applied democratic leadership style because they applied task culture in doing work. Democratic leadership suits with the task culture because everyone has the right to give suggestion and make decision.

Autocratic leadership style

Kamdar Sdn Bhd

According to Psychology.about.com says *"autocratic leadership, also known as authoritarian leadership, is a leadership style characterized by individual control over all decisions and little input from group members. Autocratic leaders typically make choices based on their own ideas and judgments and rarely accept advice from followers. Learn more about some of the characteristics, benefits and downsides of autocratic leadership."* (About.com, 2014)

Decision-making was less creative under authoritarian leadership and it is more difficult to move from an authoritarian style to a democratic style than vice versa. Abuse of this style is usually viewed as controlling, bossy, and dictatorial. Authoritarian leadership is best applied to situations where there is little time for group decision-making or where the leader is the most knowledgeable member of the group.

Democratic leadership style

Sara Lee Corporation

Meaning of democratic based on Psychology.about.com explained that democratic leadership style " *...is generally the most effective leadership style. Democratic leaders offer guidance to group members, but they also participate in the group and allow input from other group members. In Lewin's study, children in this group were less productive than the members of the authoritarian group, but their contributions were of a much higher quality."* (About.com, 2014)

Participative leaders encourage group members to participate, but retain the final say over the decision-making process. Group members feel engaged in the process and are more motivated and creative.

The differences of effectiveness of leadership style between this two organisations are authority and decision making.

	Kamdar Sdn Bhd	Sara Lee Corporation
Authority	As we can see, this company leadership style is autocratic and the authority was given to the leader or owner. A leader or owner just has the authority to decide anything.	For this company, the authority was given to everyone in a team that has formed. They are practicing participative style and their way of work conducted is a democratic style of leader and employees.
Decision making	Decision making of this company surely will be made by a leader or owner because they applied power culture that focuses on leader to make decision. It is called autocratic leadership style that relates to the scenario. Even though only a leader or owner has the right to make decision, but they have to make wise decision and think fast.	In Sara Lee Corporation, the decision making were made by team members and leader will be the mentor. So that, it is called participative style as related to the scenario. The democratic manager keep his or her employees informed about everything that affects their work shares decision making and problem solving responsibilities.

Another company applies autocratic leadership style.

"A striking example of an autocratic leader in the corporate world was Leona Helmsley of the Helmsley hotel chain. Her combative style earned her the tabloid nickname "the Queen of Mean." While Leona's autocratic leadership style did make the Helmsley hotel chain popular, her demands of perfection from everyone, and her exacting ways scraped the dignity of everyone on her payroll, from the cleaning staff to top executives. She allegedly "treated people like garbage," one example being to fire on the spot a secretary daring to use the Helmsley Palace dry cleaner to remove an accidental spill on her cloth, even though she had worked diligently for eight years." (A riview of company with autocratic leadership : part 1 of 2)

Another company applies democratic leadership style.

"OPITO The Oil & Gas Academy uses an industry-wide, employer-led Skills Forum to get feedback and input from many people in the industry. This ensures its work continues to be aligned to the changing or emerging needs of the workplace. In this, the Academy uses a proactive democratic style by providing current and relevant information about the Academy's work. It then uses a responsive democratic style by evaluating requirements for skills and training that will address the needs of the whole industry." (Autocratic and democratic - Management styles in the oil and gas industry : The Times 100)

2.2) What are the advantages of approaches to management that had been applied in both organizations? Make a comparison between both organisations.

Kamdar Sdn Bhd

Kamdar Sdn Bhd has approached **scientific management** in their organisation.

According to boundless.com, *"scientific management, or Taylorism, is a management theory that analyzes work flows to improve economic efficiency, especially labor productivity. This management theory was popular in the 1880s and 1890s in manufacturing industries and was developed by Frederick Winslow Taylor . While the terms "scientific management" and "Taylorism" are often treated as synonymous, an alternative view considers Taylorism to be the first form of scientific management. Taylorism is sometimes called the classical perspective, or a perspective that is still observed for its influence, but no longer practiced exclusively."* (Scientific management - Classical perspective : Boundless)

Advantages of scientific management to Kamdar Sdn Bhd.

1. Increase in production

   Scientific management has been responsible for steady improvements in business operations like increase production of textile fabric, school uniforms, Indian clothing of Kamdar Sdn Berhad production and many more.

2. Piecework pay system

   Payment depended on piecework basis which taken as an incentive to maximize productivity and produce high wages for the workers.

3. Early working method and control

   Scientific management involves developing a management methodology, selecting and training employees, and supervising them closely.

4. Better utilization for employees

   Scientific selection leads to better workforce which it can ensure increase in efficiency. Harmonious relationship between the workers and the management, standardization of tools, materials, techniques, equipments for increasing efficiency and reduction of production cost.

   Sara Lee Corporation

   Sara Lee Corporation has approached **open system** management in their organisation.

   "An open system refers to an entity that is provided for study or analysis. In terms of the study of an organization this is usually the whole or part of an organization. The open systems approach to management considers all organizations as open systems. It is a system that in some way or another has interaction with its surrounding environment. In other words an open system has inputs and outputs. To study an organization the following terms and definitions are outlined:

   The boundary.
   The boundary refers to an arbitrary line that outlines the area to be studied.

   The environment.

The environment includes all the aspects and influences to the area under study that are outside the identified system.

Inputs.
Inputs refer to anything that comes into the identified system from the environment. Examples of inputs include customers' orders, power supplies, technological equipment, raw material, and labour.

Processes.
Processes refer to the whole cycle that converts inputs into outputs. This includes production and planning processes as well as marketing the organization's products and completing the sales process.

Outputs.
Outputs refer to anything that leaves the identified system and is transferred to the environment. Examples of outputs include products and services but the systems approach also considers waste and losses as outputs." (Open System Approach to Management: Making it in Business)

Advantages of open system management to Sara Lee Corporation.

1. More effective problem solving

   Without clear understanding of the "big picture" of an organization, leaders tend to focus only on the behaviours and events associated with problems in the workplace, rather than on the systems and structures that caused the problems to occur in the first place. To effectively solve problems in any type of organization, it is critical to be able to identify the real causes of the problems and how to address those causes. A systems view provides clear understanding of the "big picture."

2. More effective leadership

   The most important responsibilities of a leader in Sara Lee Corporation are to set direction and to influence others to follow that direction. It is difficult to establish direction for an organization and to keep that organization on its course if you do not understand how the organization works in the first place. The leader ends up working harder, rather than smarter because they have to understand overall nature and needs of an organization.

3. More effective communication

Some of the first symptoms that an organization or consulting project is in trouble are sporadic and insufficient communications. Employees in Sara Lee Corporation need to understand the parts of an organization or project and how they relate to each other, it is difficult to know what to communicate and to whom. If the effective communication could establish, it is easy for Sara Lee Corporation to handle the organisation.

4. More effective planning.

It includes identifying desired results, what measures or outputs will indicate that those results have been achieved, what processes will produce those outputs, and what inputs are required to conduct those processes in the system.

Comparison between both organization management approaches.

The differences both of this organizations management approach is their main focus. For Kamdar Sdn Bhd, they are focusing on production efficiency while Sara Lee Corporation focus on the things related to the surrounding environment.

Kamdar Sdn Bhd focus on maximize profit for the benefit of both workers and management because they approach Taylorism or scientific for their management. So, basically the workers function is to increase productivity in consistent. They have to complete their task and will be rewarded based on their performance.

For Sara Lee Corporation, they have the interaction to the surrounding environment. They will focus everything that related with communication, problem solving, leadership and etc. By using an open system management, it will be more effective and efficient because Sara Lee Corporation applied task culture. A team with their own talent and expertise is formed to complete a task. So, they will be excellent in planning, communication with dealers or suppliers, responsible towards the organisation and many more.

2.3) What are the importance of leadership style and approaches to management to the organisations?

Importance of leadership style

Leadership style is important in an organisation because of division work. For example, if we have a leader we know what we supposed to do base on the task given that divided by leader. That is why leadership is very important thus, every organisation or firm need their own leadership style in their management. In Kamdar Sdn Bhd, they applied autocratic style which shows all decisions will be made by leader or owner.

Now, let's proceed with Sara Lee Comporation. Sara Lee Corporation applied democratic style also known as participative style. It encourages employees to be a part of the decision making. The democratic manager keep his or her employees informed about everything that affects their work, shares decision making and problem solving responsibilities. Then, democratic style contributed so much in influencing organisations planning and goals as it shows that every leader participate with their employees with the decision making.

Importance of management approaches

Management approach is also very important in organisation as it will guide the organisation or the firm. Every firm or organisation needs a good management in order to have an efficient productivity and increases profit. So, by management approach such as Taylorism is one of the ways to have a guide on how to manage the company. As referring to Kamdar Sdn Bhd they are focusing on efficiency productivity, this is a very good guidance as their company were practicing product structure. Here it shows that this company really need guidance for their company.

On top of that, management approach also important to Sara Lee Corporation. They use open system and it is quite good because they can have good interaction with surrounding environment because they focus on overall aspects. They can make effective solving problem, communication and not to forget the effective of leadership.

Conclusion

I, as a researcher for both of this company which is Kamdar Sdn Bhd and Sara Lee Corporation, I would like to conclude the structure of the organisation is very important to determine the way of work to be conducted and to know the authority in the company. For culture, it is also needed to see how the work and responsibilities being constructed in an organisation. Leadership style is to make the workers know their leader, work or task to be completed and how far the freedom of making decision. Management approaches can be the guidance of the organization or firm whether to gain the management efficiency or production efficiency or both. Overall, for the structure, culture, leadership style and management approaches are related to each other. All of these elements are the priority to all organisations to have a better management and maximization of production and profit.

For Kamdar Sdn Bhd, I would like to recommend that they should increase the motivation to the employees such as benefits, bonuses or reward for their performance and also taking care of their employees because some of the employees claiming that they were treated like machines and no accounts was taken of their abilities or their motivation. Furthermore, employees also will feel bored by doing the same task everyday because Kamdar Sdn Bhd applied scientific management. So if they take care of their employees, surely they would have increases the loyalty of their employees thus, increasing their productivity.

In Sara Lee Corporation, this company is efficient in handling the organisation. They should maintain the performing regarding structure, culture, leadership style, management approach and employee's behaviour.

References

1. *A riview of company with autocratic leadership : part 1 of 2*. (n.d.). Retrieved April 14, 2014, from Bright Hub PM Web Site: http://www.brighthubpm.com/resource management/77233 examples-of-companies-with-autocratic-leadership/

2. About.com. (2014). *Autoctratic Leadership : Psychology Definition of the Week*. Retrieved April 8, 2014, from Psychology.about.com Web Site: http://psychology.about.com/b/2012/07/13/autocratic-leadership-psychology definition-of the-week.htm

3. About.com. (2014). *Lewin's Leadership Styles : The Three Major Leadership Styles*. Retrieved April 10, 2014, from Psychology.about.com: http://psychology.about.com/od/leadership/a/leadstyles.htm

4. *Autocratic and democratic - Management styles in the oil and gas industry : The Times 100*. (n.d.).Retrieved April 14, 2014, from The Times 100 Web Site: http://businesscasestudies.co.uk/opito/management-styles-in-the-oil-and-gas industry/autocratic-and-democratic.html#axzz2z0qSsNcz

5. *Autocratic and democratic - Management styles in the oil and gas industry :The Times 100*. (n.d.).Retrieved April 14, 29014, from The Times Web Site: http://businesscasestudies.co.uk/opito/management-styles-in-the-oil-and-gas industry/autocratic-and-democratic.html#axzz2z0qSsNcz

6. *Corporate and organisational structure : The Times 100*. (n.d.). Retrieved April 1, 2014, from The Times 100 Web Site: http://businesscasestudies.co.uk/business theory/strategy/corporate and-organisational-culture.html

7. *Culture-Handy :Lindsay Sherwin*. (n.d.). Retrieved April 5, 2014, from Lindsay Sherwin Web Site:http://www.lindsay sherwin.co.uk/guide_managing_change/html_overview/05_culture_handy.htm

8. *Kamdar Group (M) Berhad | Malaysia : Internet securities Inc*. (n.d.). Retrieved April 3, 2014, from Internet securities Inc. Web Site: http://www.securities.com/Public/companyprofile/MY/Kamdar_Group__M__Berhad_ n_2039950.html

9.Lindsay Sherwin. (n.d.). *Culture - Handy : Lindsay Sherwin.* Retrieved April 3, 2014, from Lindsay Sherwin Web Site: http://www.lindsay sherwin.co.uk/guide_managing_change/html_overview/05_culture_handy.htm

10.New Charter University. (2011-2014). *Attitude, Behaviour and Perceptions : Organizational Behavior.* Retrieved April 7, 2014, from Organizational Behavior: https://new.edu/resources/understanding-people-at-work-individual-differences-and perception--3

11.*Open System Approach to Management: Making it in Business.* (n.d.). Retrieved April 14, 2014,from Making it in Business Web Site: https://suite.io/maureen-cutajar/3ysz2mv

12.*Organisational structure* . (n.d.). Retrieved April 5, 2014, from uir.unisa.ac.za web site: http://uir.unisa.ac.za/bitstream/handle/10500/1133/03chapter2.pdf?sequence=2

13.*Product departmentalization : BusinessDictionary.* (n.d.). Retrieved April 1, 2014, from BusinessDictionary Web Site: http://www.businessdictionary.com/definition/product departmentalization.html#ixzz2PBrxsKMZ

14.*Scientific management - Classical perspective : Boundless.* (n.d.). Retrieved April 14, 2014, from Boundless Web Site: https://www.boundless.com/management/organizational theory/classical perspective/scientific-management-taylor-and-the-gilbreths/

YOUR KNOWLEDGE HAS VALUE

- We will publish your bachelor's and
  master's thesis, essays and papers

- Your own eBook and book -
  sold worldwide in all relevant shops

- Earn money with each sale

Upload your text at www.GRIN.com
and publish for free